LATOGENEIA

THE POETRY OF ATHENADORUS

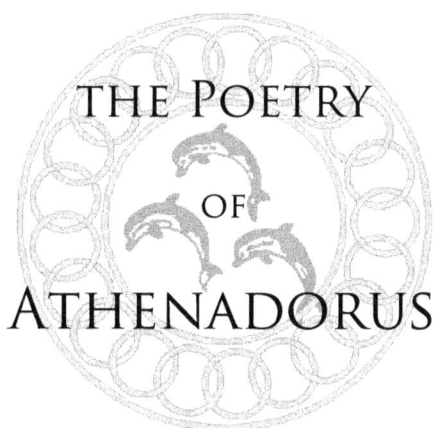

DANAAN PRESS™

RICHARDSON, TEXAS

EY 5.3005 - 5.3035

𖤍𖤏𖤐𖤑𖤒𖤓𖤔𖤕𖤖𖤗𖤘 𖤙𖤚
𖤛𖤜𖤝

Library of Congress CIP Number: 96-086551
ISBN-10: 1-890000-04-3
ISBN-13: 978-1-890000-04-2
DANAAN PRESS ID: 001-0510-02120-8

CONTENTS

Preface

LATOGENEIA is a volume of my poetry, written over a period of more than thirty years. The topics of these poems range from a celebration of the Goddess's gift of human relationships, to nature, to civic pride, to haiku, to (some rather undisguised) homoerotic peregrinations.

The Latogeneia—that born of Leto or *Latona* (name of the Goddess as Mother of Artemis and Apollo)—is a celebration of one Danaan's life. The association of this volume's title with Apollo, the joyful male among the nine Muses, is appropriate, for the first poem, *Prologue,* starts, "The Nine ethereal Muses I sing...". Yet, lest one forget that my name means "the gift of Athena"—as indeed all Life is the gift of the Great Goddess—not only have I included THE PRIME IMPERATIVE and THE THIRTEEN FREEDOMS, but I also wrote the poem *Prologue* to finish with a stanza commemorating the verses used at the close of each of the three *Phædran Letters* (central section of *The Athenadoran Library*):

ATHENA, Goddess, Great and True,
Sister, Mother and Dame, no few,
Builder of Cities, Creator, to You
This song will I sing, and all other ones, too.

— Ἀθηνάδωρος

THE PRIME IMPERATIVE

↰3 The **Prime Imperative** is that which all nitrogen-based life must obey: that each living entity will live its life in such a way as to maximize the survival chances of Life itself.

There are three constituent Imperatives which, in balance, *are* the Prime Imperative: that one will live its life so as to maximize the survival chances of one's species (*The Natural Imperative*), one's identity group (*The Social Imperative*), and one's self (*The Personal Imperative*).

The **Prime Imperative** is also called the *Contract of Life* or the *Natural Contract*, for, in receiving the gift of Life, proteins and their more advancing forms abide by this requirement called the *Prime Imperative*, established by the Goddess at the very birth of the Universe.

There are Thirteen Freedoms which we Danaans hold to be absolutely essential for humans, for them to be able to follow the **Prime Imperative** fully and freely. These thirteen are the social expression of the operative basis of the **Prime Imperative.**

–Definition of the *Prime Imperative*, taken from
Athenadorus's *First Phædran Letter.*

THE THIRTEEN FREEDOMS OF THE DANAANS

1 **FREEDOM OF THOUGHT**: that no government shall attempt to control the minds or mental processes of its people.

2 **FREEDOM OF RELIGION**: that no government shall attempt to establish one religion over another.

3 **FREEDOM OF SPEECH**: that no government shall attempt to stifle the free expression and communication of ideas, or the publication of the truth.

4 **FREEDOM OF ASSEMBLY**: that no government shall limit the right and/or ability of the people peacefully to assemble for just and reasonable purpose.

5 **FREEDOM OF PETITION**: that no government shall limit the ability of the people to address themselves to that government for redress of ills and grievances.

6 **FREEDOM OF POLITICAL ASSOCIATION**: that no government shall attempt to infringe on the right of the people to express alternative viewpoints, publicly or through suffrage, or to form associations for the peaceful furtherance of those viewpoints. Nor shall a government restrict suffrage so as to deny any people their right of alternative expression.

7 **FREEDOM OF PERSONAL IDENTITY**: that no government shall take upon itself the right or power to assign or enforce gender roles, careers or attitudes; to legislate prejudicial discrimination; to legislate moralities; to deprive individuals of ultimate control over their own bodies; or to interfere with the private, non-violent activities of consenting adults.

8 **FREEDOM OF PERSONAL SECURITY**: that no government shall disregard the right of the people to be secure in their persons, effects and property, both real and personal , against unwarranted searches, seizures or any other action of that government without public, free and just due process of the law. Nor shall any government abridge the people's right to own and hold private property.

9 **FREEDOM OF PERSONAL INITIATIVE**: that no government shall deny the people, as individuals in equality, the right to strive for the betterment of their lives or conditions of life, in moving forward to the goal of emotional, physical and financial independence, which is the basis of all hope in human life, and of all progress in human society.

10 **FREEDOM FROM HUNGER**: that a society must be responsible for the prevention of hunger among its people.

11 **FREEDOM FROM DESTITUTION**: that a society must be responsible for the prevention of want for basic necessities among its people.

12 **FREEDOM FROM FEAR**: that a society must exercise its powers and abilities to restrain its government from actions and laws that are detrimental to liberty, to inspire that government to enact legislation which will encourage justice and responsibility, and which will discourage violence among its people.

13 **FREEDOM FROM IGNORANCE**: that a society must exert itself fully in striving to educate its people; and must work to diminish the effects and influence of those who espouse ignorance.

–Exposition of the *Thirteen Freedoms of the Danaans*,
from Athenadorus's *First Phædran Letter*.

Prologue

The Nine ethereal Muses I sing,
Whose favored glance, our guide,
They bring to nurture human life: love and joy,
To give us gifts of mind, heart and hand,
Build bonds of friendship through all lands,
Gossamer ties of caring respect—
Knowledge and understanding.

The Three of the Three of the One I sing,
The Cephisian Muse, Nine-Unity:
ATHENA, Goddess, Greatest and Best:
My life, my love and all the rest of
A universe of vital delights to You,
All-Muse, Creator, Great and True,
These songs I sing and all other ones, too.

Dedication:

Jeffrey Alexander Qualls
EY 5.2996.X.3 – 3031.VIII.5

ἄγγελος ἀπαράκλητος

when the heart sees
what the mind cannot grasp

when the sudden chill moves
the warmth to shudder and gasp

when spirit guides our steps
where coolest logic cannot map

there we feel the gentle clasp
of the hand, of the unsummoned angel,
attentive, day

and night

EY 5.3035.I.21

DON'T VEX THE VIKING
Únáðið Ekki Víkinginn

You knowingly drive the wrong way
Down a well-marked one-way street and wonder
Why I call the cops?

Don't vex the Viking!

You leave an animal in a
Sweltering, shut-up car and wonder
Why I call animal control?

Don't vex the Viking!

You're stuck to that cell phone, yacking,
Texting and weaving the lanes, yet wonder
Why you're cussed in four languages flat?

Don't vex the Viking!

You drive by a crowd of my friends,
Yell *Faggots!* and, speeding away, wonder
How that trash-can came crashing
Through your car window?

Don't vex the Viking!

If you cannot exercise public decency and respect
For the members of our human community, and curb
Your religious bigotry, superstition and hate, then don't wonder
That Lindisfarne (793) was not that long ago:

Don't vex the Viking!

When someone of power, intellect, presence and skill
Far greater than yours is the target of your stupidity,
Then don't wonder when the very lesson you get to learn is

Never vex a Viking!

EY 5.3032.VIII.27

Denk' ich an Deutschland in der Nacht...
(The Austin Poem)

It has been so trying long
since last I saw You, Lady,
You who are watchful
of the City in the night,
so many months long past
since last my eyes free
caressed Your form standing
stark against a sky deep endless
in its so soul-robbing blue.
How You cradled me in the warmth
of friends' boundless understanding,
where my pains were my joy,
to be blind was to see,
to be among the citizens was
to know the very best
of humanity's growing glory.

From the far-distant waste
I see You, brilliant white in
radiant midnight mist—a beacon
in the Great Land's golden midst—and
cannot control the tears:
for the heart in exile
never ceases to weep—
for bluebonnet-scented dreams,
for life and loves and liberty
left behind, in the City
that was his own.

I return to You, Bright Lady,
for I must see the tricolors float
above the Legation's flowered grounds,
the Lone Star reflected in the
Colorado's gentle flow: for Austin
is Texas's heart and soul—
and Texas is Life itself.

EY 5.3004.XI.20

Infiniti—

to have seen eyes-dancing
to have wanted, reached out,
yet, shy, afraid,
to have remained still,
still wanting

to have watched you-desiring
to have searched, been found,
yet, cautious caution's hoping
to have reached longingly
toward longing eyes-dancing,
blue-grey tender in far-distant singing

to have slept with arms, enraptured,
tightly wrapt around the world,
to have awakened—
and kissed the dawn

EY 5.3004.X.11

rêve

Il y avait une bicyclette
sur laquelle, au bois,
je l'ai trouvé—
un rêve
aux cheveux blonds.
(Est-ce qu'il y a d'autre?)
Nous bavardions, 's'en sommes allés,
avons fait l'amour
et là, je l'ai trouvé encore,
cet homme, aux cheveux blonds—
un rêve
sur bicyclette.

Maintenant, il s'en est allé
au bord de la mer,
aux bras d'un autre.
Et moi?
Je m'en vais en rêve.

EY 5.3003.IX.18

dream

There was a bicycle
on which, in the woods,
I found him —
a dream
with blond hair.
(Is there any other kind?)
We chatted, we left,
we made love
and there, I found him again,
this man, with blond hair —
a dream
on bicycle.

Now, he is gone away
to the edge of the sea,
to the arms of another.
And me?
I'm going into a dream.

AUSTEX: J. E.

I had driven from Dallas, two hundred miles,
unable to suppress those vagrant smiles of
the River City's quick liberation.
So much, so many, the room so full
yet empty until I saw that you, leaning
aimless against a vacant bar, had
arrived, the lustrous, wondrous star of
screen and stage and wet, wet dream.
Last weekend across the blonds and bares,
I dared to look, to dream, to stare
at sparkling eyes shining in the glare of lights
reflected from your dark hair's shimmers and heights
of desire and sensuous, desperate delight:
Miss Breck done proud, my libido to spite:
tonight.   You stood at the bar: I lusted, remote,
though I was there, right at your side, chomping on ice—
I just had no device that would allow me to repeat
those phrases so trite that echo cross-country
every night with every meeting, every slight.
I would rather not know you than know just this:
that my legs, my muscles, my smile,
the whole list, that what they import/export
does not warrant a kiss, does not even summon a friendly hand:
I'd rather be one of those in the band of your
lovers and admirers who have seen from afar
the wonder and style that
make you a star.

But I hate little cars that take you away.
Oh once, just once, please say hello
and stay.

EY 5.3002

Eyes

Lover's eyes so soft and bright
Reflect across the depths of night
And morning's sweet caresses, where
Lightning glances from touch to
Touch
Of swelling satisfaction

The whole Earth spreads Herself before
To offer joy and pleasure—but there
Is none anywhere for me, except
Your eyes' dark sweltering treasure

Ice

It's impossible to drive
with tears in your eyes
and ice on the windshield
from the cold of others' hearts

So many lonely people in the world:
why did I have to be one?
Why did I have to need others so strongly,
just to be left to freeze?

To learn to kindle the
Fire Within:
to cherish, yet in loving,
allow to live free

EY 5.2996

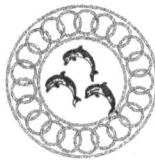

sheets

sheets press cold against
naked flesh
pillow kisses one head
where two were before

your shadow dances
across the bluebonnet meadows
of my dreams
late night feasts
late morning love
the joy of you deep inside

so far away, yet
so tender close

the porpoise's kiss
the morning son
gone too soon—once,
over the river; now,
beyond the forest,
away

EY 5.3003.IV.17

Skip

the nights
of holding my own hand—
of caressing my own thigh
and its being someone else

of squeezing the
hard-throbbing heart
of desire
for that man
that man with the vein
in his arm
always protruding
pulsing
piercing my night
with the silence of his cries

I put my soul around
engulf
the entirety of his life
feel the dancing beat
of his heart's gyrations

take me take me Oh
for Zeus Apollo Hermes
Narcissus's sake
take me
beyond the clouds
of my desire
beyond the clouds

EY 5.2999

first love: JJA

My soul overturns each time
I see you, no matter when,
no matter where.
Yet, how can I tell you just
how I feel?
Especially the sensations
when I see you smile,
hear your voice,
see how the sunlight changes your
jet-black hair to silver.
But, what do I say?

It is so difficult to tell someone you love him.
Far easier to ignore him:
far easier to learn not to feel.
Where is the tenderness,
the understanding, the compassion?
They are within us,
waiting.

EY 5.2996

VNN 82

On the patio—what a sight!
Even through all the brew—
I saw you that night—
and knew I had to have you,

You, with that blond
who kept dancing with everyone else,
You, with eyes as big as New Jersey
and a face that would melt
a Minnesota snowstorm
or an Arkansan's heart,

you, a Gemini's dream
whose long moon-legs dropped
around you and drew you in,
tight, deep, secure,
Pisces, and hot,

you, so nervous about the arrival of
another, who is ready to depart,
even though so strong, so ardent
you grasp, cleave, desire,
because you love and you hope—
the way I did—
we are such dopes, who could share
our soft affections' compassions,
but must wait to thrive,
to live, love wisely:
learn how to survive.

"We just moved in."
Big shit! So what?
He's all ready to go!
And you and I know—
we're not!

EY 5.3003

worth more than he knows:
Worth, More than He Knows

a new, glorious sun spins gold in the bare limbs of
the trees on the eastern edge of the pond,
gilding the tall dry grass at the shore,
scattering shadows across the ice,
which glitters and glistens when the morning's
glacial blasts contort the trees
and the golden grass slaps at my knees.

we're so far from each other—you there
in the rain—me standing in the frost—
yet the cold cannot touch me, for I
am lost in the warmth of memories
and desire.
I feel your arms around me again, as
on our first night, when warm enraptured,
I suddenly awoke
to be not afraid of love, when the world
turned and smiled.
I look over and see your profile sculpted
against my pillow in the cool morning light,
feel the hair of your broad chest
on the soft underside of my arm: watch your eyes,
feel you breathe, hold you tight.
I see you leaning against a column,
tall, handsome, sexy, aloof—
this first moment I saw you, I remember it so well,
how my heart started pounding, when you finally spoke
to me
and I knew you were the most beautiful man
I could ever hope to see.

the crows call from the western forest's edge
and over the knoll, the clanging bell tells
the herd is on its way.
the sun climbs high in the cold December sky
and I walk slowly to the house across the fields
where my car waits, impatient,
for the long journey home.

EY 5.3004.I.1

Here #1

here I sit
in a vacant grey room and,
fool that I am,
I wait.
alone with my thoughts,
with desperation,
killing the hope
my love begs to dare.
I do not prosper when left in silence
nor blooms my love when abandoned to die.
when life holds nothing but ignoring snores
and deceiving diversions,
I alone lift my dreams
toward the sky

Here #2

here I am, alone again:
the box talks at me, through me,
around me,
but it doesn't listen
and I know it doesn't care

where is the man that used to be?
the man who loved my touch
why does he hide his private skies—
am I so dangerous
to illusions—must I be kept away
from rainbows that are no more?
or am I no more and do rainbows live
and are true men just shadowed shades?
where is the man who shared my life—
my evenings, days and delights?
he's far beyond the rainbowed sky
and I am the prisoner of night

EY 5.3002

Joshua, Jesus and the Evening News

Our evening wind burns still hot and dry,
the mediterranean sun frees cooling shadows
vagrant across houses yellow-reddening
through the aura of suppers' preparation.

The soldiers rush through the gates,
surprise, horror and strangling fear:
death marching to yells and cries
and screams of terror coming near.

The old push the children,
mother-hen them away;
the young desperate search,
reach frantic for weapons,
find none—they were taken
by warriors just sent away.

Grab the screaming toddler from its
grey grandmother's lifeless arms.
See the sword part the skin,
the blood spurt out, the ribs
crack and crunch as the
blade scrapes through to silence.

See the teenager running,
never mind his broad bronze shoulders
and sun-blinding smile:
one leaden lump to the left of the spine,
he raises the dust as he falls.

Grab the cowering teenager from
behind the concealing divan,
never see her wide sweet lips
and eternal deep brown eyes:
one shot above the ear,
blood spatters your uniform.
Red on green and it's christmas again.

See the young mother frenzied
for the baby left asleep.
Her neck breaks, so easy,
and she's nervous no more.
The child slobbers, grins, gurgles,
reaches out—

Grab its ankles, sling it hard,
hear its skull gentle crush
as its head hits the wall:
the cartilage and new bone break
and plunge deep into its brain.
Baby blood flows so crimson bright
down the whitewashed wall—
its body quakes, shivers, spasms,
drains its life on the hard dirt floor.

The Moon now rises, claims the sky
to carry the tears of Humanity's cry of
MURDER: innocent life destroyed:
of blood-and-dirt caked babies'
chubby hands' spasm-grasping at the
tattered robe of Death.
The Moon cries out for Justice,
Justice, Justice!
Will anyone hear Her call?

The heat and terror brought by the day
refuse to leave: skull shadows of might.
And Palestine sleeps fretful
in the pallid palm of night.

EY 5.3004.X.21

For around nine days in the fall of 1982, while driving the 60 miles three times a week between Hot Springs and Little Rock, Arkansas, I felt the presence of an infant lying on my chest: it was bloody and cold, and I was overtaken by paroxysms of grief. This was written during that week, the week in which the world had not yet discovered the massacre by Christian militia of the women, children, sick and elderly of the Sabra and Shattila refugee camps.

Sanguis in manibus Jovis et quisnam nunc Jehovem servaret...

Ann's haiku

west of mountain peak

a hawk darts—no—autumn leaf

jumps, joyous for flight

EY 5.3004.XII.1

Autumn dawns on the road to Little Rock

I.

dragon's breath clouds lie

thick on dragon-back mountains—

fire-mist in the east

II.

sleeping-dragon grey

veils hide the fresh-born phantom

pale cold-rising sun

III.

bleak sky ice-crisp blue

reddens with leaves—as I drive—

home-dreams westward fly

EY 5.3004.XII.21

松山俳句

しょうざんはいく – *Shō-zan Hai-ku*

Pine Mountain Haiku

一 *ichi*

peaceful is the tree

deeply rooted in our soul:

no peace wants of death

二 *ni*

birds-on-clothes-lines clouds

quick hide the sun's face when its

cool becomes cold wind

三 *san*

hill-top trees standing

stark, black spiny scaffolds, still

against dark grey skies

四　*yon*

rain falling in sheets
so soon changes into sleet—
birds perch, long for flight

五　*go*

snow drifts through bare limbs
soft, cold-quilting ev'rything:
tree-haunting spirits

六　*roku*

green leaves burst from buds
among the forest flowers'
deep cloud-mountain vales

七　*nana*

in woods bluebird sings;

its echoes run ev'rywhere—

after, strolls silence

八　*hachi*

robins fly to nest:

bright sun changes to mist light,

pale moon in the night

九　*ku*

love is the bright light

warming golden paths of peace:

death brings no darkness

EY 5.2993

wind: 1

the warm wind winds down
over the towering mountains and vaults
through the flitting shadows of the deep,
green wood, into the golden
sunlight, glowing down from its
far-away forebear in the clear vacant
blue sky, as the rustling
yellow-brown grass bows in deep
respect to its visitor, who
has seen so much and traveled
so far, but stays only a second,
to vanish

wind: 2

pitch black, swirling clouds
drown the sun in darkness freezing.
the driving rain washes the trees
and the wind sends waves of leaves
panicking across the dead brown grass:
they leap toward heaven, flying frantic sorties
over shivering shrubs and coward-bushes.
the fire in the fireplace pops.

wind: 3

the wind softly filters through
the willow's cascading hair.
mountainous clouds gather,
creating valleys that send pink and purple
shadows through the sky.
the heavens bend to touch the
verdant, peaceful Earth
and darkness blankets the land

EY 5.2992

FRAGMENTA

Fragment 1

mockingbird sings in the
palm tree fronds waving soft
in the breezes of the night ...

half-moon shimmers blue-white
behind cotton-lace cloud curtain
carried on the fresh-windy northwest ...

mockingbird keeps me company with
its lonely repertoire, flowing thin
over the waves of the pool, tranquil,
cool as the notes, hovering
echoes in the midnight air ...

you sing to the Moon
and I sing to you,
unrequited melodies, sung
to those who, far away ...

EY 5.3004

Fragment 2

one-thirty monday night
I could sleep with
Tennessee but he has dreams
of one in Japan
and I am in lust with a world
who stands behind the bar,
with blue eyes ...

Fragment 3

... blond on stallion back .....
..... dusty boots and work-sweaty shirt ...
....
.... biting through the denim ...

Fragment 4

Why is love so warm
and yet so cold?
Brilliant within long
unexpected moments,
like snowflakes falling
among raindrops?

Why ..... snowflakes
melt ....
............like
lips touching wine ...

Fragment 5

When did I first love you?
I could as easily tell
the moment the world coalesced:
for I did not love you suddenly,
but, as I know when it is dawn,
I knew I loved you.
Dawn has no abrupt beginning ...
... and merely appears, diaphanous, ...
... its blossoms sweet moistly unfold ...

Fragment 6

a bristly brawling autumn wind
kidnaps the trembling leaves
and frantics over the cloudy-green lake
until the hydros heaves in
white bearded spray ...

fat bluejays play in the living towers
and chant their wavering keys,
from pines and oaks majestically swaying ...
... great thick branches lofty ...
..... with grey-furred jumping ...

Fragment 7

... misty grey waters above ...
I stand ... great ancient rock:
below, houses mill among high trees.
a fog blanket pulls itself away from
the deep-blue ribbon in the distance,
while the bustling wind runs flailing
to the top of the mountain, leaps off,
glides down into the forests below,
whose bows rise and fall as rich foliage ...
suffocation into ..... breath ...
of Life ....
... the sudden moist-fragrant coolness of night ...

Fragment 8

nothing surpasses sinking
in mountains of golden
honeysuckle-blossoms ...
... to the birds who,
joyful at the approach of
spring .... their
sweetest notes in .....
celebration ....
... my love ...
....
... and I burn with desire ...

Fragment 9

..... Austin, Texas .....
... heaven ....
..... in an orange bathrobe ...

Fragment 10

cold was the .....
... and dusk amid shadows darker.....
... walk along the deserted street.
The wind against my back goes
right through my coat,
chilling me to button it up.
Down the street a dusty grey cat
falls off his trash can and bolts terrified
across the street to the shadow elms.
I walk up under a lamp-post and
lean against it: try to draw warmth from
its beams. It doesn't help.
Then I see you before me ...
... the cold is no more ...
.... warmth flows ...
..... happiness .....
... from your eyes ...

Fragment 11

... his still-wet swimsuit
in my hand ...

Fragment 12

... when in the hazel-moon western sky
the Evening Star has found Her bright
lunar throne, then .... assured
of the Queen of Heaven's abiding Love ...
.....
... civilization new-blooming ...

Fragment 13

.... for you
are Humanity: Builder of Worlds ...
...

EY 5.3005

W.M.

it is always startling,
amazing, disarming, the sight
of eleven-eleven on the clock,
in dark or light, or dim
or bright, being carried
to Warren's Tennessee moment of life,
and how he would wake me,
tight blond smiling
in the middle of the night...

EY 5.3016

THE ROBB POEMS

Robb 1

how have I now gone
from clarity to
heart-pounding uncertainty
from equivocation to
heart-rending yearning
from strong self-assuredness to
heart-piercing desire?

your eyes dance,
shimmering,
like the morning mist
joyous
across the verdant meadows
of my mind.

Robb 2

have I seen you sleeping, softly,
cool against my warm chest wrapt
in the sheets
of my mind?

have I held you tightly, dreaming,
cool against my warm legs wrapt
in the sheets
of my mind?

have I kissed you sighing, deeply,
hot against my body wrapt
in the sheets
of my mind?

did I dream you,
blond child into man?
yet if not a dream,
why does it seem,
you arise from the torrid depths
of my soul?

you will awake one night,
with lights leaking 'round the drapes,
you will awake with a start
from a dream of ancient origin
and you will know that
dream's embodiment
is me.

Robb 3

to forget my lips on his cool shoulder
in the warm depths of the night

to forget the effervescence of his
sparkling eyes deep staring into mine

to forget how his hello
shatters all goodbyes

so then cry that
tempest of unseen tears

to quell the burning
ache of these muscled arms
yearning to hold

the man I cannot see
the man I cannot touch
the man I cannot forget

EY 5.3014.IX.3

RB 1

pillow, pillow, vacant pillow
so whose head did you gentle hold
that night of my remembering

pillow, pillow, empty pillow
now whose hair did you smooth caress
those hours of my remembrance

pillow, pillow, barren pillow
then whose ears did you breathily kiss
that dawn of my golden treasure

pillow, pillow, lonely pillow
why do you weep,
you who have sung
the concord of mellifluous souls,
harmonic stillness of the night

now comfort find—
conjure the image
of my desire,
and savor the radiance
of his smile

RB 2

river keeper, water spirit,
evoker of creative flood

the tides surge forth
on feeling your voice

and touching your hand
makes bloom the vibrant desert
of desire

RB 3

I see the Bobby,
the Bobby sees me.

How pleasant just to stand
here in your kitchen door

To talk freely here and there,
touch subjects of here and there, and there
to catch sight of laughing eyes gleaming
in the morning light

To touch without touching
and, afar,
feel you near:
be silent to hear you sigh
as you sleep

I see the Bobby,
the Bobby sees me.

And I do not want to wake.

EY 5.3014.IX.7

Visit

I did not see you this year, Texas,
bright in broad blue-bonnet gingham fields
and far-soft brown-eyed lowing

I did not feel the first nipping frost,
in the eastern wilderness
Nor that cold central spring

I did not share the streaking wonders
of the far west desert's dusk
Nor the gentle Gulf-coast dawn

I visit, yet know no return—
I ache: I cannot leave,
yet cannot hope to stay—
must hasten back to a distant Bay
to complete the solemn journey

But in my mind's too vivid eye,
I see that white star floats high,
lone and free,
and beckons home to me

EY 5.3005

The Inner Bell
For C.C.

The City and the bridges glimmer bright
from across the severing Bay, the west wind
blows but soft up the grassy hillside—
a warm sunny, sleepy afternoon—
I lie back and stare at the sky

I hear it afar, from the forest glade,
one note, at one round, even, tenor pitch,
piercing the foliage, which sighs in the singing
of a cool noon breeze

I move toward it as again it sounds,
its single, plaintive, searching note,
reach a sparkling rushing stream, its
solar glints adding to the flashing backs
of turtle, tadpole and silver trout—
it tolls again, toward the top of the hill—
I run: at the top it entones once more,
sounding on, up the mountain,
toward the sky

In the high mountain's rich grassy meadow,
my ears ache from straining so hard to hear
what direction, what source, what song,
what band have joined to make this
soul-searing, searching sound

Again—from the east, it knells,
sounding clear from the face
of the rising Moon, radiant ivory pale
among the ebbing, opening veils of the
setting sun's pink and purple rays—
and the cool valley's calling owl—

The peal reverberates from east to west,
then back to front and through again,
filling the sky, the land, the light

with ever increasing, booming flight—till
it drones, it penetrates, it knells
through me—connects all things
in transcendant unity: Earth, Sun and Moon,
all that exists, All Life is One!
Be One with Life! entones the Inner Bell

I awake in the stark sunshine
of warm autumn's summery day:
mourning doves coo and bill and sway
as the west wind tosses the trees—
and while I watch the doves swoop
to the sidewalk, search for seeds,
it tolls again, that bell I had heard,
on the mountain amid the forests of my mind:
filling the sky of my soul—
it rings with the sweet pureness of
innocent understanding, it rings
with the peace which loving acceptance
can only bring: the Love for the Life of the Living

In the search for knowledge, wisdom,
the peace in understanding,
I walk through the Forest
and I listen for the Bell—
for, let uncertainties be as uncertainties will,
the Inner Bell always rings True

EY 5.3006.X.24
EY 5.3008.IV.5

how long

how long, O Goddess,
must I mourn

in the midst of lucent happiness
I am shrouded in the inner cloak
of sorrow,
and conceal the visage of loss

for I am reft of more friends,
brothers, sisters and cousins
than most will ever possess
or caress

and I cannot cease to mourn

EY 5.3014.XI.27

www.ingramcontent.com/pod-product-compliance
Lightning Source LLC
Chambersburg PA
CBHW071744090426
42738CB00011B/2566